CW01023088

Ex Libris

poems by

DAVID HUGHES

edited with an introduction by

ANTONY DUNN

Valley Press

First published in 2015 by Valley Press
Woodend, The Crescent, Scarborough, YO11 2PW
www.valleypressuk.com

First edition, first printing (October 2015)

ISBN 978-1-908853-54-7
Cat. no. VP0059

A CIP record for this book is available from the British Library.

Printed and bound in Great Britain by
TJ International Ltd, Padstow, Cornwall.

www.valleypressuk.com/authors/davidhughes

Contents

but no-one seems to be listening

Introduction

David Hughes wasn't my teacher. He taught English literature and language, from 1975 to 2004, at St Peter's School, York, where I boarded from 1986 to 1991. He was my friend, though, and he showed me that I could love poetry – generous enough with his spare time to spend long evenings talking to me about poems by Ted Hughes, Edward Thomas and the other Great War poets, and criticizing teenage proto-poems of my own.

I was conscious that he was a poet himself, albeit a diffident one, modest about his writing, and I don't remember him showing me any of his poems at that point. If notes in his papers are to be believed, he submitted few poems to magazines, anthologies and competitions – and the submissions he did make were, for the most part, local to Yorkshire. There's no indication that he ever submitted a book-length typescript to any publisher. After his death, when his family delivered his papers to me, I experienced a curious sense that I was uncovering some important secrets about someone I'd loved, and thought I'd known better.

It wasn't – isn't – a huge body of work; a little over two hundred poems which, as far as I can be sure, David believed to be finished. His preoccupations are clear – the impact of war upon the individual, the landscapes of mountainous and glacial northern Europe, the ecology of school, his friends, Wales, Liverpool, York, moments of communal celebration (this collection begins and ends with Christmas poems), the eulogy. On the one hand, it's a poem's responsibility to speak for itself; on the other, there are some features of this collection which might benefit from a little privileged insight.

What I didn't realise until some time after meeting him was that, in autumn 1986, I had first encountered David very shortly after one of two pivotal events which would shape his poetry.

In July 1986 Barry Daniel, David's friend and colleague, was killed in an accident on the Austerdalsisen, an arm of Norway's second largest glacier, Svartisen. Barry was leading an expedition of students from St Peter's School, with David one of two other staff members in the party. Barry, in attempting to rescue one of the party who had slipped into a crevasse, became trapped himself. David was unable to save him, and Barry was dead by the time he was taken from the crevasse by a rescue-helicopter crew.

This accident became a weight which, perhaps, the readers of David's poetry best understood. A clutch of poems from August 1986 were included in a collection of accounts of the incident by various members of the expedition, and 'Valediction' was one of ten poems submitted to, and published in, *Burning The Old Boys*, an anthology of poems by students and teachers from St Peter's, in 1992.

In August 2004 his time as a teacher at St Peter's came to an end as he struggled with alcoholism – drinking, according to a number of friends, as a means of coping with what he himself described as his post-traumatic stress. He continued to write – steeping himself in historical research about railways, the internet, the two World Wars (even a cultural and historical study of lavender, while writing copy for a website) – but a second crucial event provoked another slew of poems which, opposite the dozen poems inspired by Barry Daniel's death, represent the other pole of this selection.

As David himself wrote in a letter to his friend and erstwhile pupil, Matthew Hodgson, in October 2010:

'I was sort of invited to write a history of a pub, The Little John in Castlegate. I was sitting in there with my laptop on a few occasions and a young glass-collector /

odd-job-lad got chatting to me – and I to him. […] He is interested in many of the things I enjoy – mountaineering / sketching and painting / railway history; and, it eventually transpired, poetry. His name is David […] leading, understandably to us being known as young Dave and old Dave.

'*He has a bad past – whichever side you take. He was 19 when I met him, and had been in Care […] Anyway, I don't know the whole sequence of his past […] but by the time I met him, he had offended again after leaving care, sufficiently to be on probation […] and living in a 'care' hostel […] And it was going wrong. He's not a naturally compliant young man. But I did like him (I still do), and got on well with his friends; and by the time it came to New Year 2008, I offered him the spare room here […] and he said yes.*

'*It was a good arrangement – so it seemed. His girl came to lodge as well for a while. Trouble was, then in early summer she left him; and he lost the plot, […] And one evening at the very end of July he came back here when I wasn't really expecting it, and I made some remark which triggered his anger. To walk away from the argument, I went to bed. But that action – I am told – only wound him up the more. He brought up a kitchen knife and cut my throat. Not badly, just a short, superficial cut; but (as with such wounds) there was enough blood to cause some of the others in the house to call police and ambulance – and then suddenly it was all out of my hands. By the time I was allowed back out of Casualty (it was not worth going: even if you find it hard to visualise me without a beard, I have cut myself shaving much more bloodily) the lad who fled the house in the immediate aftermath was walking back to say sorry, and promptly got arrested. He did not even know that he had cut me.*'

'Young Dave', convicted of the attack in 2008, served six months of a twelve-month sentence in HMP Hull, during which time he corresponded often with 'Old Dave' and the prison poems began to take shape.

> 'when he was inside he asked me to send him stuff of mine that he had been reading here; and then he suggested there might be stuff to write about what was happening to both of us 'now'. He was right. If you can make a valid separation, he has been providing the inspiration while I have given the perspiration'
> (Letter to Matthew Hodgson, 25 Oct 2010)

As early as February 2009, David was e-mailing me drafts of the 'prison poems', and a handwritten letter from, and signed by, both Daves accompanies a small selection of the prison poems (some with titles later changed) sent to David's parents on 14 June 2009. These prison poems, collected under David's own title, 'but no-one seems to be listening', were unusual in that David seems to have been genuinely ambitious on their behalf, determined to have them published. In a letter to Sally Evans at *Poetry Scotland*, who did publish four of them in spring 2011, he wrote,

> 'If you do chose [sic] to publish them, Young David and I very much wish to see them attributed to both of us [...] The shared nature of their compostion [sic] is seen in the way that 'the things I miss' and 'It's time for you to be my Simon Yates' are spoken by young David's persona, and the other two spoken by old David.'

The week commencing 21 November 2010 was National Prisons Week, as David had remarked in a letter to his friend John Jacobs that month, which also included this:

'One of the humbling things about the whole situation be-
tween me and young Dave has been seeing your reactions
and others to what I did after David knifed me, telling
me about my quality of forgiveness – which is difficult
espcially [sic] *because I don't really comprehend it in*
those terms at all.

'I find it quite difficult to get my head around it. I sup-
pose that is because I always thought of 'forgiveness' as
something difficult which has to be worked towards. But
for me, there was no action or re-action to David knifing
me, just an acceptance of something which had happened,
just my natural reaction.

'I don't think it is a false modesty, to feel that I don't
deserve to be given credit for forgiving Dave, any more
than I deserve credit for having two legs when I stand up
and walk. It was just something which happened without
me thinking about it.'

Many of David's poems are very personal – gifts to specific
individuals – which, in some cases, leads them into senti-
mental territory. More than a few of the poems among his
papers were omitted from this collection for that very reason.
They were private communications, probably never intended
for a wider audience.

Curiously, a small number of those personal gift-poems ap-
pear in his papers under various titles, and with various dedi-
catees – a repurposing which, given the shortage of clues as to
the dates of composition of most of the poems, was one of the
more vexing challenges in the editing of this collection.

David wrote very little poetry in the years after 2004, but
the period from 2009 onwards seemed to mark a revival of his
enthusiasm for writing, performing and even publishing.

At the 2010 Malton Literature Festival, he read a selection
of new poems from a cycle (as he called it himself) called

'Whitby and the Great War'. This new work told two stories about the Yorkshire coastal town; that of the wrecking there of the hospital ship *Rohilla* in 1914, and that of the shelling of the town by two battle-cruisers of the German High Seas Fleet in December of the same year. He was clearly as excited about this project as he was about 'but no-one seems to be listening', and excited to have presented some of its poems to an audience whose response was very positive. The Whitby poems are excluded from this collection partly because of their sheer mass, and partly because they attempt something so different from the rest of these poems that they would have unbalanced *Ex Libris*. They will find a space of their own.

David was diagnosed with bowel cancer in summer 2011 and died in December. In the intervening months, he talked for the first time about his anxiety that his poems might be lost. His friend and colleague, Paddy Stephen, recalls conversations in which, despite his life-long reticence about pushing his poems out, David expressed a forlorn hope that someone other than himself, after his death, might usher the poems into a public space – a task which, for all his renewed vigour, for all the meticulous arrangement of his papers before his death, for all the time (albeit, too little) he had to prepare, he didn't feel able to attempt himself.

Here they are, then, outliving.

My thanks are due to the family of David Hughes, Gwilym in particular, for their trust; to Thia Daniel for her generous advice; to Paddy Stephen and Ian Lowe for their confidence; to Kate Ross for her assistance with the preparation of this collection; to Jamie McGarry of Valley Press for his enthusiasm; and to Matthew Hollis for his wisdom.

Antony Dunn
September 2015

Ex Libris

1957

It is Christmas, always this afternoon,
always the same, always Christmas
afternoon, after the Speech: full,
we are walking it off on the Prom
where today my own children scatter
around me. My skirt ripples and pulls

in the breeze. My headscarf blows.
Below Frodsham Hill I see the twin
slow-meeting arms of the arc of the bridge
at Runcorn, replacing the old Transporter.
When I call him David comes to look
at the one half-sunken cycle in the mud

and I turn west here to face the falling
light, looking at Bidston Hill and those sad
masts of ships, riding out the ebb,
their lights sharp and green under the Welsh sky,
suddenly aware, gathering the children,
what I am waiting for. David is five.

When I was five my father sailed out west.

Glan yr Afon

I walk into this strange farmyard, feeling I belong
at the height of my father's waist, holding his hand
and gazing up at rooftops under the trees. In the distance a
   clang

of metal frightens me, echoing off the barn
while I stumble on weeds and cobbles. 'Behind
that wall,' he is telling me, 'a long time ago, I was born,'

and I cannot grasp the meaning of so much time
before me being alive, because I am already seven:
his childhood is like a story in my mind, and the tame

horses circle and circle the pump of the well
in a buzz of flies and sweat over water, even
though the scum is inches thick now, and the windows
   bricked up in the wall.

'Half a world away'

Half a world away
and half a world apart
my parents were already quarrelling.

I picked up the phone
and found nothing there
except a blurred and nervous crackling

then a distant voice
saying in slow English
'will you ring him again, please. Keep ringing

again. I will pay'
and a number I knew was my own,
setting the earpiece singing.

'*Iach y da*, I stutter from my exile'

Iach y da, I stutter from my exile;
Or *Borra da y chwi* and a wary smile.
The clouds drive past the cottages. The rain
Mists out the mountainsides. I'm home again
And wondering, as the track resolves itself
From dark and rocks above me shelf on shelf,
How *hwyl* and *hubris* come to be combined
In me, in teaching. Up this hill I'll find
The chapel that my great grandfather led;
And out along the cliff beyond the head
-land by the wreck, the lifeboat slip
-way from which uncles brave the tides' strong rip:
Their bodies and their spirits in this place
Confronting real problems face to face.

'I think that I have seen'

I think that I have seen (I am not certain:
Perhaps I am inventing) a Sunderland flying-boat
In my imagination. But surely the aircraft
Is behind the camera? – banking steeply

So that somewhere pinned above its windows
On the green depths of a monochrome sea
Armed merchant ships are moving peacefully
Across the still wartime photograph

Much earlier, in a crowded corridor,
Above the sawn-off leather of a window-strap,
Among tangles of rucksacks and startlingly
Young faces peering up at blacked-out stations

I see Durham Cathedral, like a water-colour
Before the war in railway train compartments;
Then the Tyne, and in Edinburgh rain
And steam, and presently the Forth Bridge

This side of Rosyth where I shake from sleep
And recognise my father in snapshots
Of groups in uniforms or civvies, not unlike
I had imagined him – on those parades

Or dodging breakers on the promenades;
And then being briefed; and wondering perhaps
If I his yet-to-be-imagined son
Might understand him sixty years away.

'Teacher'

The most surprising fact of this
was my surprise.

I know if he'd been working
I'd have been at work,
but hearing they were going to operate
I went, needing this visit,
knowing it could be the last.

When I arrived his bed was empty
and the nurse said, 'No
but try the private rooms…'
while all my confidence
went even from the surface
and I followed voices
out along the ward,

until I listened for a moment
to a classroom silence
turning the rattle of hospital metal
into the clatter of a school canteen,
heard his question, heard
the pupil's hesitant answer, heard
the lesson of my father's operation
patiently explained
to someone urgently admitted
for the same.

'God damn this racking cough'

God damn this racking cough… no joke… I do
Remember York… recall my friends… Will you
– Please – tell them (if you see them) I would write
Except I can't control my hands. Tonight
The trembling's getting bad. It's cold… The best
That I could scribble is my name. The rest…
They made it up… I never did those things
They've stretched me into owning to. I'll swing
In any case   alive – until my heart
Is gutted from my chest. *They* wrote my part…
I did my best… but in the end I'm stripped
Of dignity… identity… the script…
Betrayed my friends… and cause… I don't know why…
Scorching me from 'Guido' down to 'Guy'.

'I dream briefly of riding tall'

Every Peterite should feel an almost personal interest in the Battle
of Marston Moor: on the day of fighting George Wandesforde set
off towards York in order to get his schoolboy brother safely away.
And he happily met him riding out of town to see the fight…
riding towards the moor with other boys [from St Peter's], which
was going in their simplicity to see the battle.

I dream briefly of riding tall
in the mist, past the straggling trees
of the ditch cut, waterlogged land,
conscious of the danger, sensing
beyond the next skyline massed cavalry –
Cromwell's horse at Tockwith – and seeing
behind me Newcastle's cornets showing brave;
beyond that, somewhere, Rupert dining untimely;
and the sudden blare of trumpets and horses.

But the memorial, modern and mundane,
says everything: reduces to critical comment
all their strategy.
                    Only the bulleted trees
and the country's deepest grave, conscientiously noted
and faintly recalled from my history books,
make the battle real and people the darkness
with ghosts: the full moon on Long Marston
fills the shadows with something more solid than truth.

I turn back to my teaching, aware
that the pupils in front of me now
would just as easily leave their books,
make their way across country, watch men die,
tend the wounded, and come back to lessons tomorrow
as if they had learned nothing.

French Trip

The café holds in its shadow five boys
cradling drinks in an unfamiliar world
seen friendlier through the bottom of each glass.
In the street the day passes.
On the clock-tower marking Vendôme and this square
rooks step from ledges in a drunken fall
to glide while around them the doves circle
and clap their wings in gentle laughter
on the springtime roller-coaster of the sky.

Watched by his friends and the café patron
hours later, on his knees searching for change
but losing much more than he finds,
the first has had more than enough.
What he throws is less solid than dignity,
already gone. Around him the others applaud,
pissing themselves in drink and laughter;
then know it's time to go, finding themselves
suddenly more strange even than the place.

Late evening in their beds and sleeping bags
the other four share drinks and smoke, swigging
good wine, settling the day into their sleep.
His vomit curdles warmly, and they help.
When they carried him in he was like a puppet
or a doll, loose-limbed, stuffed with rags. His eyes
open but scarcely see. His throat and gut
gag. His world is sick and shakes; but inside
something has flowered which will never close.

'I knew you as a strong, self-counselled man'

I knew you as a strong, self-counselled man.
You kept yourself for self, and hid or showed
Your choices for the best; and then allowed
Even your friends to guess. You tried to plan
The times for study, sleep, and even thought.
Where honesty was called for, you declared
What many would keep secret. Those you taught
Admired or hated you, but never cared
Enough to try to know you better than
This. If any did, then you would pause,
Maintain your isolation.
                                    But I can
No longer keep distant from you, because
I saw the blood that stains your bathroom sink.
Your life is much more open than you think.

Christmas, Easter, Summer: ends of term

and suddenly landscapes
will open, so always
around me are rocks,
steep ground and thin gullies;
inside me, insistent, the fear,
and the need of wide spaces.
This time it is Glencoe,

Stob Corrie an Lochan,
behind The Three Sisters;
and always a roaring
which wanders, diminishes,
surges, and goes with
the wind on the buttress
until we've ascended

far up, past the freeze-line
to slate-grey and whiteness
where only our breathing
will heighten the silence;
and round us the knowledge
that here in this corrie,
next month, with the Spring,

will be running of water.

Hafod

15 December 1980

Watching Andy on a bunk,
bowed over his boots, applying
water-proofing, holding off
the weather, tomorrow, and the steady
press of the world, the blur
of television voices in the other room;
the curled head and shadowed eyes,
yesterday's tiredness, and all
the work. Some of the looks are returned,
becoming smiles: some of the evening is shared.

December on Snowdon

Above the ridge we rested in the lee
Of the summit hotel, from wind-borne drift
That hurled against the peak across valleys
We saw only in snatches, late and early,

Between the clouds. We descended from cairn
To cairn. The path confirmed itself, *the Ranger*,
The walk, cautious then conversational
In your relaxed and easy company.

Now, as always, night closes round the hut.
People settle to cards, or cooking, while
My thoughts, like flocks yesterday gathered
From the snow, come together, leaving the hills.

Glyderau

16 December 1989

It was dusk in the gully, slowly deepening
To dark on steeper snow, each rope-pitch lengthening
Exposure to the cold. We climbed out, meeting you
On the plateau at last. Mist shredded off in gold,
Magenta, blue across the pinnacles. The old
Day died in splendour. Sunset. Far out west, we knew
They were *cloud*-mountains like the first explorers saw,
And, far above us, through the cloud-wrack, one bright star.

Nant Ffrancon

We may have picked our ways along this deep valley
For centuries now: although water holds the floor
And rock is its border, everywhere else there are
Traces; tracks, ways, pack-horse steps and paths not wholly
Eroded, not only abandoned to the sheep
Whose browsings rib each slope. Perhaps the tourists' cars
Pack each layby, while the nature trails and footpaths
Are becoming overwhelmed. But above these the steep
Places, rock buttresses, high plateaus, sharp ridges,
Bright llyns of water, cloud, and the sudden edges
Hold our memories, draw our dreams, and compel us
Upwards, high, whatever the valley might tell us.

Sudden Storm

High on Braeriach plateau, walking north, we watch
Dark river down the gulleys, and that whole great cleft
Obscures with mist. We work to safeguard our descent

And concentrate until, when we look up too late,
There's no world left, except a roaring, snow-swirled cone
Of wind and torchlight, outside which we – somewhere – left

The tents eight hours ago. Although the map would say
The track is clear, the Lairig narrow, running north
And south, this sudden storm is throwing night and ice

Across our faces till our breaths begin to freeze
Into our hoods, snow goggles glaze, becoming masks
Of plated frost, and compass needles disappear

Out at the hand-held limits of our sight. White noise
Distracts me when I try to count my steps. I strive
To sense my feet enough to let them feel the path

I know, its snow-clogged fall and rise through boulder-fields.
High on the ridge, imagined avalanches boom
And fall. Until, at last, a lull clears all the air

For headtorch beams to search and sweep, revealing prints
Across a slope which make us think, *that's it! We're there!*
We're not: *we're here*. These are our own, the first time round.

Much gentler flakes begin to lift across this col,
And we must turn to look ahead once more because
We know, at least, it can not take long now. Night thins.

Not far above us here, a cold, reprieving moon
Begins to shine through cloud that's shredding off
The ridge, the Lairig Ghru, the Pools of Dee, our tents.

Time at Gwastadnant

for Tom Whitcher
August 1996

Conceive of this: *collision of two continents...*
Red, Rhyolitic tuffs are spread, slow-motion soft
In submarine, volcanic-cauldron heat – across
A syncline in which sediments accumulate.
Interpret thus the dipping strata of Twll Du
And Cwm Glas Uchaf glowing in the evening light.

Uplift. Whole geologic ages make a gentle plain,
Eroding smoothly from a curving ridge, perhaps
Four thousand feet above Gwastadnant, where we camp
Imagining *Pre-Cambrian, Quaternary...*
Such time-beyond our grasp in this tranquillity;
A mountain-scene whose lines we trace... *Pleistocene:*

A glacier-stream beneath the ice-sheet cuts across
Southeast – northwest, reshapes it all to what we know;
Erodes and deepens hanging cwms where there were dips
Between soft spurs; truncates obstructing rock to crag;
Bull-dozes debris and moraine along its trough
And leaves raw rock exposed to freeze-thaw shattering.

Millennia: x-thousand years for ice to work
To water on the land, knife-edging Crib Goch Ridge
To crag and pinnacle; each winter time and spring
Accelerating scree towards the cwm, the Pass;
Where boulders crumble into rocks, to stones, to soil;
And liquid seeps from damp, to flow, to stream, to this

Pool deep enough for swimming, in the shade of trees
Where insects dance, star-speckles up-sun in the eyes
Of one exploring water and sharp stones – who finds
Red, Crib Goch Rhyolite; who stands *two thousand feet*
Below that ridge; who turns with sunlight on his back…
The young man lifts his hand, and smiles, and waves to me.

For Mark, off *Cemetery Gates*

2 August 1991

Resuscitation Room: first Andy, sitting still
in climbing vest and tracksuit; then Simon
whose salopettes and right hand melted on your rope
to brake you, their faces showing distance, and
regret at having seen you plunge so fast, so far
from them, and us, before you slowed, were stopped
– until you sink again, perhaps this time
beyond our reaching or recovery. All evening
blood is draining through your wounds, is draining
from the day in slow diminishments of hope
while we find clues in silences, long waiting,
stillness at last, hanging on for now, and sleep.

Intensive Care: visiting you in no-man's land
we watch the signs we scarce know how to read:
the blotchiness of urine in that tube, the drip
of saline, lung-blood seeping in the bag, the hiss
of oxygen as you respire, the trace of your heart-beat
hesitating on a screen above the precarious ledge
of your bed, one wry, slow wink, one brief caress:
just holding on is enough… Your pulse steadies out
at eighty six awake, or ten beats less asleep;
and soon, it eases gently when you see us smiling at you
from our places at your beside. What we treasure now,
days later, is that sharp, green line: *your life*.

'Late summer bivouac'

Late summer bivouac, high on Glyder, prizing
Both your friendships. Clear in my memory now, far
Peaks purple westward, recede into velvet dark.
Ridge beyond ridge, the plateau's outlines blur;
Summit rocks grow tenebrous. High above, we mark
The all-night swinging splendour of the Milky Way;
Silent, smooth-sweeping satellites; one shooting star;
Harsh, silver-flooding moonlight in the hollow
Early hours below Castell y Gwynt, where we lie
Talking at first, watching, dozing, sleeping shallow
Above thin, pastel-shaded mist; until the sky
Grows light, first touching Snowdon,
                                    Then the Sun –
                                            Rising.

'What am I longing for'

What am I longing for
down in the lowlands this hot August day –
hills I might climb?

Is it something I saw
from the valley here where men are gathering hay –
is this a sign?

What do I want to do
striding along the ridge to reach the crest –
just climb up high?

or is walking with you
enough to explain my love of all the rest –
does this say why?

Cwm Idwal

I live all seasons here –
All years and months, starlight and storm,
Clear August moonshine, spindrift-filled New Year,
Lake-surface-stripping wind, hand-tearing rock still warm

At midnight after drought,
Or skimmed with *verglas*, winter's glaze
On which my cramponed boots will skid about
Like some ice-skater's nightmare. One day I shall laze

Among huge-bouldered scree,
Or dawdle to the ridge around
The upper cwm in swirling mist, to be
Alone on rock, in space, in this air's sound

– And stay until I dare
Take one step more. I want to go
Beyond experience on this crag. Out there
In Hanging Garden Gulley, *Snowdon Lilies* grow.

Ingólfur Arnarson, in Smokey Bay

It is the fish, whatever
the wind, I remember, east
carrying a stench of fish rotting
on the eyes, and west the dusty edge
of fish drying on racks on the ness.

But it was not so
at the start: when we first landed
snow buntings in a cloud
lifted, and circled the totems,
driftwood shuddering our run
up the beach. Out to the left
two rivers steamed and I could not believe
how their waters scalded
my leap in Reykjavík.

Moonstones

1944

There was rain on the hills,
mist in the fjords, streams
in the gutters of the bleak unmetalled roads,
snow briefly on the intake and a boy
in a shop when I was going
to Leirvik with my boots
leaking and my uniform
soaked with the weather
and my sweat.

He fixed my boots
and held the weather off.

1979

Go from Gotu to Leirvik on the road
where I take the snow-plough.

Buy bread there, which you will like.
Look in the water to see whales.

Go to Fuglafjordur. There is a path
to walk to Hellur. Follow the way

to Oyndarfjordur where you must see
the Moonstones, which you will like.

III. POSTCARD FROM HELLUR

1979

We came to Hellur on the pack-horse track,
the lads and me. There's not much traffic since
the motor-road got through. We climbed the ridge,
and rested by the cairn to see the view.
Across the fjord, Öyndarfjordur lies. The cliffs
on Kalsoy tower and cut the cloud: the low
Atlantic sky breaks blue. We wandered down.
We're looking for some legendary stones.

IV. VILLAGERS OF OYNDARFJORDUR

C. 1600

I watched them coming,
the raiding party closing on our rock-cut quay
where the iron post marks the deepest landing.
Our boats were wrecked, and foundered in the bay

The wind that helped the Frenchmen burn us here
kept all our hope aground in Elduvik.
The villagers at Hellur did not dare
approach: the sky and bay were thick

with level smoke and level, clinging cloud.
I could not see Blaborg or Husafell.
Kalsoy is close, but *they* were in the sound.
I saw no place to turn, no help.

v. 'I STOOD ON TINDUR, BUT I COULD NOT WATCH'

I stood on Tindur, but I could not watch
the plunder going on below the mist
that shredded past me like a nightmare's edge.
The wind was gathering above the ridge
behind my home. The cloud was torn across
the bay by Kalsoy's cliffs. The pirate ships
rode anchor in our lee. Two boats –
no more – came up against the quay.
I heard the flames when Oyndarfjordur burned
a sacrifice to blinder gods than ours.
I heard the curse.

VI. THE MOONSTONES, OYNDARFJORDUR

With stealth of rat and cowardice of dog
the raiding party brought the sudden hiss
of flames and falling rain. Their wakes
engraved the bay with latticed agony.
They raped the women and enchained the men.

The witch on Tindur cursed them as they left;
and hard against the quay, astonishing,
their boats remain, as rocks, that rock
still moored. The tethered string pulls tight,
goes slack, pulls tight, with each advancing and
receding wave. The hanging stone chips flakes,
confirms the movement.
                              Jacob showed us this.

I lesstofan af skolarkennari ur Skogur

[in the Schoolmaster's study at Skogur]

When I stoop in the turf-walled house
by the quiet church in Skogur
and enter the schoolmaster's room,
his desk faces me under the window.
His books wait for me in their glass case
to tell me how little I know.

In Iceland, mountain slopes may become 'active' because

[a] Freeze-thaw action breaks apart fractured or unconsolidated lava-beds from other, more solidly bedded, sediments.

[b] Earthquakes, small but frequent, shake loose friable volcanic deposits or existing scree.

[c] All stone is frightened of height. Large basalt blocks are particularly cowardly, and fling themselves without notice downward from isolated positions.

[d] Rock groups display a natural tendency towards depression. Stones isolated at the edges of beds become particularly suicidal.

[e] Trolls on ridges, otherwise frustrated of their prey, employ volunteers from groups [c] and [d] as boulders to bombard travellers in the valleys below them.

'Ten years ago, near fish racks behind the frozen beaches'

Ten years ago, near fish racks behind the frozen beaches
Of Akureyri, or icicles along the frozen streets
In Reykjavík, where I walked watching snow
Fall in lamp-glow or swirl in blizzards whose depth
I could know only by the light or not-light
Of an airport beacon on the city's water-tanks
I invented acquaintance with you,

And wrote my first *Letter from Iceland*,
Describing men with snowploughs and shovels
Clearing the runways and duck-lakes of drift,
Telling of wind-blown trees with Christmas lights
On ships in harbour from storms, or under the moon
And a long aurora, and thought it was fiction.
Then I returned to find our friendship true.

Iceland… in place of Myths

Dulled by the North, I wait
For landfall, far beyond Faeroe,
Itself furthest, feeling
Seas steep and falling into
Troughs; anticipate the sea-
Sick hope of landfall, the first,
On Iceland – which is real,
More firm than the ship,
More solid than sky
That scuds above us like curtains, clouding
My memory of otherwhere. This place
I locate by your being here.
In the breaks between the squalls I'm sure
I'm secure: I watch the north-
Running waves. I feel and hear
The wind. Slowly the harbour grows.

We will gather on deck, armed only
With cameras and anticipation –
No language – not intending
To go further than our wits
And our wheels will take us,
Hoping to gain nothing but memories
In place of looking forwards,
Realities in place of Myths,
And understanding how the legends grew.
This is what I offer
With my love for you.

Christmas Present

We only stopped to camp there once: that night –
An undistinguished northern Iceland site
Of lakeside pebble, silt, and starving grass.
It fronted on grey water then, and greyer cloud;
And over twenty years I think I can recall
Snow-gullies up the mist on high, grey cliffs.

Next morning we extended breakfast: Simon and
Garfunkel and Cat Stevens' Greatest Hits are still
Evocative: still, *Baby, it's a Wild World*
In which *The Sound of Silence* echoes on and on…

That afternoon, above steep harbour steps, we shopped
For sweets, not tasted in ten days, and souvenirs
Of grey Icelandic wool. So what comes back to me
From all of this comes back for you, and all this comes
From you – and all of this you taught me: how to buy
Those presents, how to want to buy, to want to give,

While all your greater music still encircles me
Today as then, beyond our camp site, half beyond
The edge of sleep and memory, an all-night, long-
Day lasting, dislocated, celebratory
Lament – like all the dispossessed, yet still
Belonging, where we camped beside that lake,
Around an oystercatcher's nest, beneath the ridge,
Together, always, in my less-than-perfect memory.

'When I see, clear as this'

When I see, clear as this,
Hveragerdi and Stokkseryi
Under the aurora I want to watch
The past coming to meet us
For ever beyond Ingolfsfjall
On streams of lava and ice.

The Troll Wall: Romsdal, Norway

Sea-level: for the shadowed valley floor no sun
is ever high enough until the hills wear down.
Eight hundred metres: clouds hang on the tree-held screes.
Twelve hundred metres: overhanging rock, the summit ridge
Come into sunlight as the day swings on; light plays on
 pinnacles.

On the shadow line the early mist disperses,
burning off in the sun. The shade grows more intense
among the higher rocks: eyes and beards take shape.
In winter when the weather worsens and I travel alone
I will remember this, beginning to believe that trolls are real.

New Year's Eve

On the last day of the old year

on the margin of Reykjavík Bay,
level shadows, sunrise at noon,
snow, snow-buntings and the salt-cleared
strand of the beach; by smooth water
under a pale sky, past boats with Christmas trees

I walked until the light went down
to a full moon with seabirds and soft water,
slush in the rock pools, ice on the sea-wall;
across the bay the silhouette of hills:
the Snæfellsjökull, and the Northern Lights.

New Year's Day – Norway

Last night, I knew I would remember it for years;
a green aurora curtained all the midnight sky
behind the snow-limned ridge: a New Year *Polar Lys*.
I slip and sidestep through this Arctic afternoon,
cross-country ski-ing to a distant, wood-built farm
in dwarf-birch scrub and scree beneath that ridge. There,
    soon,
we will be eating cakes and drinking English tea,
illuminated, for the first time in my life,
by candle light like magic on their Christmas tree.

Summit Ridge

Coming up Trollvegen, swinging hairpins
into a blur of low clouds and high waterfall
we arrived, early, midnight, half in light
with the boys stumbling, cold-cramped, tired
and bleary in the back of the minibus.

Mid morning, creaking down a board-walk
past tourists to that precarious viewpoint
above Trollstigheim, there were five of us
thinking, *we must look like real climbers*
with rock behind us in their photographs,

before we clambered steadily from lowland
three times into valleys higher than the cols
between capped peaks, lurching left-handed
round floe-covered, clouded lakes where terns fed
in splashes of white against the glacial slate.

Off rocks at last, we roped, and crunched blue footsteps
over snowfields where whiteness developed to glare,
struggling out through clouds, finding a clear sky
while mists of sweat and heavy condensation
blurred our goggles and made our suncream run.

I remember my fingers as sticky as toffee but slick,
not gripping on the wrappers of our chocolate bars
when we ate where spiders struggled against altitude
across spores of lichen; and a veil of midges columned
gently in the still evening air, as we went on.

Unmeasurably far off between the white and blue,
almost-black prows and superstructures, distant, huge
outlines, anchored in the drift, hulls of ships
whose bow-waves lifted in a froth of water, summits
in a sea of cloud where we became cloud-walkers

out onto rock again: that vast arête, a skyline
whose dreadful figures, sun-trapped, fossilise
in the preservation of old myths: Trolltind; Troll Wall;
and us: stunned by sun and glory on this edge.

What falls from here will free-fall for a mile.

As Was, As Is

I knew that I would never climb with him again.
Ten years ago, this was. We'd bivouaced in rain
on Liathach, and in the cold, cloud-shrouded dawn
he made me lead. It took more talent than I had.
He simply followed while I lost us – twice – going down
the wrong damned ridges. Camped, at last, I could not hide
my fury, cursed him that he'd made me fail his test
in front of all the pupils, told him I was fucked
if I'd put up with that. The end. I still can taste
the pride I felt, in anger, that I had not faked
not minding what he'd done. I hadn't ever claimed
great things for my ability, or routes I'd climbed.

I think we disagreed on something every time:
ten years of strong opinions which we would not tame –
and, always, my conviction that I'd had enough
of being disregarded: wanting to retreat
from Ben Macdhui when the wind was like a knife,
but pressing on; or knowing that we should go straight
across that sodden col on Skye he took us round;
being sure that finding Dafydd's top meant aiming left,
and (rightly) being guided right; on days it rained,
suggesting I could use a rest (he always laughed)…
Yet in the end each time I knew that I would need
him and the hills again, and could not stay annoyed.

A disagreement every time until the last.
High up on Svartisen that night, without the least
resemblance of a row, we sat and talked till late
about our next objectives – going down the ice,
or out along the ridge – until the Arctic light

was cold and blue around us, while I watched his face
grow calm and settled, concentrating, almost grave
but full of humour when I caught him in the pose
of one last photograph, perhaps the best. I grieve
for our next day: the deep crevasse; the desperate pause
while helpers came; that sudden chill; the tears; the pain
of knowing none would ever climb with him again.

I listened carefully

I listened carefully to what was said
through tears and silences those long half-light
half-dark six hours we first knew you were dead:
we told our stories many times that night.

Yet still I cannot picture you dragged out,
rope round your ankles, feet appearing first,
fists clenched, eyes closed, jaw slack as if to shout:
perhaps, for me, not being there was worst.

Instead my grief is ambushed by small things:
the anti-freeze drained from your camera-back,
those battered crampons, harness and stained slings,
your unsmashed altimeter, and the sack

your wife sent up with extra clothes and rope,
her sack, too small to carry so much hope.

Crib Goch Ridge

Some days above long drops I cannot bear
to watch you move. However much I know

you're strong and skilled and climbing safely there
still my imagination sees you go

in tumbling arcs across the shattered air,
and hears you breaking on the rocks below.

Crib Goch today is not like that: we walk
the ridge almost with hands in pockets, high

on more than altitude, enjoying talk,
and silence, and exposure, you and I.

One steps between us suddenly. You balk
and turn away. I need not wonder why:

I watch you look to see how far the fall
will take him when he trips, then turn to me

and nod your head, to say *I know*. That's all.
So much. Both of us knowing lets us be

at ease with one another, helps me call
the fear we share our *love*. It sets us free.

'It doesn't happen every night, but sometimes'

It doesn't happen every night, but sometimes; dreams
of being back in that tomb-cold crevasse – fast caught,
with no equipment left – disturb my sleep. My screams
(I think) are silent; and although the rope is taut
above me, pulling it's no use: more falls. There seems
an endless coil up there; and when I fight, no thought
coheres in all that sense of loss. The blue ice gleams,
hard-trembling while I writhe until I wake, distraught.

'I surface gently, swimming up through dreams'

7 April 1987

I surface gently, swimming up through dreams
that wash and tremble past me into light
from unfamiliar windows, whites and creams,
rough-textured, cold, uneven walls. The night
ends placidly. My bedroom floorboards creak
while I dress slowly, wondering how to say
the poems which I feel.
                      This time last week
I rose an hour ago and climbed all day.

Valediction

for Barry Daniel

Perfection, where all things are fixed and true?
It doesn't sound the kind of heaven to strike
you dumb with wonder: you'd have nowt to do.

You'd much prefer a heaven where gods might hike
on sponsored walks that you could organise –
to build a climbing wall, or something like.

Your sort of heaven should have lowering skies
that always look like rain, but never quite
make up their minds – then soak you by surprise

and leave you squelching in your tent all night
with sodden sleeping bag and wrinkled feet,
damp boots, wet breeches, shrinking till they're tight.

When morning hammers in with wind and sleet,
disgusting though it seems, your flapping tent
must feel a bit like heaven: twelve square feet

comparatively dry, where you're content
to fester till they call you. Then in haste
you'll shudder into clothes: it's time you went.

I hope your lunch is always Lion Bar waste
or green fruit pastilles – nowhere near a stream
to swill away their sickly after-taste.

It won't take much of those to make it seem
that reindeer paté, marmalade and bread
are things you've never eaten, just a dream.

But dreams aren't things confined to food or bed:
your waking, walking dreams inspired us all
to want to follow paths you chose and led –

and led us safely till your own one fall,
your fatal stumble where our paths all fork.
I mostly hope your heaven holds lands that call

where all their better bits are three months' walk
through glaciated valleys, peak on peak,
that shadow, loom and avalanche; and talk

must always plan in detail, week by week,
the many first ascents that wait for you:
those marvellous, untrod summits you still seek.

'David, I shall take you to where'

David, I shall take you to where
We might sip snowfall in hollows
While brief flakes meld to solid chunks;
   sweet taste of tears on cheeks

Steep tumbling compressions of white
Are creaking between that vast ridge
And the deep blue of crevasses:
   bright figure vanishing

You will stand on the headland there;
Scent fresh winds and the stinging, fine
Dry dust blown over hot moraines:
   grief sweating through my skin

Listen to ice open fissures,
Split and wrench scree from the mountain,
Rumble of avalanche and stone:
   slight trembles of weeping

Flesh-tearing, hard-frozen iron
Grinds hillsides now and for ever
Unrelenting: ice-cap glacier
   surrounded by absence

Through which the third will walk always
Beside us when there are only
You and I together, alone
   with stories to tell.

Summer 1913

How confidently they were photographed:
The young Head Master and fourteen of his boys
(An Umpire, a Scorer, the team and one reserve);
How confidently they were all described,
That common, extra-ordinary team.

BASKETT
who was 'a good field', stopped a shot he should have
    dropped
but it is not known where: there is nothing in the book
(though the Scorer survived, having more than the usual
    luck).

HARPLEY
who 'guessed too much on the off' can have 'hardly made
as many runs as expected': he felt obliged to 'go in first'
a third, a fourth, – too many times until the worst…

HAYNES
who later made up his mind, as advised, for a shortened run
and made it through in the end to the Western Front's
front rank, there 'made runs that were badly wanted', got run
    out.

NELSON
had been 'deadly' on the drying wickets of summer 'thirteen,
but must have envied his namesake much in the next few
    seasons
of war in drenching fields and swamps, much deadlier
    regions.

PATTINSON
whose cricketing promise was never fulfilled, for all his
    experience,
though he'd been a brilliant and safe hockey 'keeper not
    long before,
must, I fear, have rushed out once too often during the war.

RICHARDS
always played straight but had too little life to improve:
he took pains with more than his cricket, and kept his eye
on more than the ball, but was stiff, and learned to die.

TENNANT
who soon earned his dashing place on terribly other fields,
played most games well, his cricket being not the worst;
had two more birthdays: died on his twenty-first.

Seven of the players down by Armistice Day –
And even the slender boy in the Umpire's coat,
Yes, even the Umpire lost his cheerful name
By the end of the War by being Jolly dead.

The night wind brushes past the world,

taking all its colour;
outlining bulk; and leaving sense of shape;
monochrome hills;
absence incomprehensible;
movement of boys
whose
lights
hold off the end of day

whose only 'lights out' is sunset;
whose only curtains are
a dusk of branches on the upland edge;
night skies; dark trees;
distance indistinguishable;
noise of waters;
lights –
lights –

and wind beneath the stars.

East of Ypres: Sanctuary Wood

November night in Sanctuary Wood: the broken Old
    Contemptibles
have re-assembled in the low ridge lee, where field-gun
    shrapnel
tears the year's last foliage from trees that splinter, till it
    seems there'll never be
a spring sprung green again. Soldiers, sleeping shallow
    under leaf-mould,

move uneasily to nightmare falls of shadow and the falling
    fire
of flare-light, or to their own falls in fire-fights; while
    soldiers' clinking webbing-
metal mingles with the clanging hoofs along the Menin
    Road this long
exhausted night. Yes, soldiers, shelter here, where trunks of
    trees embed

hot shards of shells, until sweet April sunlight tries to
    brighten all the day
but brings you rain, such gargling rain the enemy will bail
    and guide and gutter
down your trench. First blossom now, apple, cherry, white-
    thorn, haw-thorn,
loads the boughs, and foot-falls finely, silently like flakes of
    freshest snow

upon the hasty graves we dug amongst these groves, where
    shreds of uniform
mock thinning shrouds of washed-off soil: your whitened
    skulls beneath the skin.

Lochnagar Crater

La Boisselle Village
Summer 1999

then and now meet
west of the crater where
fragments of bone,

a named razor
and his rusted helmet
exhume themselves

Edward Thomas, 5th February 1917

after 'Adlestrop'

[from the War Diary]   *'At 7 a.m. after many stops and starts we were close under partly wooded chalk hills, among railway trucks, and near a village with here and there an upper storey quite open like a loft. Snow. Gradually flatter and poplars regular as telegraph poles, orchards, level crossings, children. Buchy at 10 a.m. – Y.M.C.A. – Leave train. Nearly lost train. Fine snow-fall. Furzy cuttings. Mistletoe in field, poplars by Alaincourt. Amiens at 2 and train left a score of men behind for a time. Pale sky and crimson sun at sunset. Doullens at 8. Guns all the time…'*

Yes, I remember Alaincourt –
The name, because one cold spring day
Of sleet, the slow troop train drew up there
In sunlight, unexpectedly.

The steam hissed. Someone cleared his throat.
No one left and no one came
On the bare platform. What I saw
Was Alaincourt – only the name

And poplars at the village end,
And mistletoe in a field. Snow lay
Among the railway tracks, as pale
As the cold, crimson, sunset sky.

And for that minute a field gun sang
Close by, and round it, as deadly,
Duller and duller, all the guns
Of Flanders and of Picardy.

At the Grave of Edward Thomas

Many maps have led me here, many books brought me
to this moment between two villages: Agny
and Achicourt. It rains. I've come at last to see,

(perhaps to understand) one grave: Edward Thomas,
Poet, (row C, stone forty three), last November's
poppies, and 'Old Man' planted in the chalky soil.

Humid, all about me the warm air cracks then flaps
as if it remembers huge bombardments only
to replay them obsessively, thunderously.

This green lane, half path, half stream, skirts familiar ground,
the back gardens and allotments of my childhood,
rising gently to a wet lawn under cool trees

where I wipe rain from my face, read the register,
take pictures (anything except pause to listen
for his voice in the unbetraying songs of birds),

wander past dull stones, until suddenly 'Bayer'
stops me – a Bavarian, laid here for ten months
before the sunlit, cold, quiet April moment

Second Lieutenant P.E. Thomas was brought in
from Beaurains, almost unmarked. This feels like coming
home; and as I sense it, fresh drops start to fall.

Hedd Wyn of the Black Chair

who died on Iron Cross Ridge in Belgium
on 31 July 1917

Hedd Wyn: I fear you find your shining peace
At 0-three hundred zero hours, this dawn
Just west of Pilkem, where no words will hold
Your meanings now, or life. *They*'re posted home
With some Lieutenant-censor's note to Birkenhead's
Eisteddfod and your fame *a'r Gadair Ddu…*

Before the Chair, they'll call for you three times –
Twice, and again – as 'Fleur de Lys', to take
The Bardic throne for which they have prepared
A black sheet that will drape it like a shroud
Or shroud it like a drape… or like the blinds
Which now black out the windows of your farm

Where Evan, your father, wishes only you
Might know for now what everyone now knows
But you. And at the ceremony, my great-aunt's
Young husband's younger brother is a boy
Who holds back tears but who will one day carve
For you some eighty years too late your poet's face

In grey Ffestiniog slate on Iron Cross Ridge…

at the Junction of Mill Road and St Pierre Divion Lane:

'The Pope's Nose'

1 July 1998

Here's where the difficulty was, exactly here,
where I am standing with my back to the ploughed slopes
on which so many thousands died. Their silent ghosts
call to me to re-turn, to watch them breast the bags,
clamber *over the top*, break woodenly into
their lumbering runs, come on, and then go down in sheaves
each time the gunner catches them. *His* concrete nest
is ruined at my feet; and when I bend to scruff
my hand across the clay surrounding it, I find
the stuff I take for root and bramble catches me.
Its barbs are rust-encrusted now, and on their twists
the oxide flakes to ochre surfaces, as if
this German wire itself still holds, and weeps, their blood.

The Last Post

Thiepval Monument to the Missing
Easter 1999

When the bugler sounds it is – we should know –
A lie, but tearfully alluring. All around us
In a wider silence, their carved names scroll
On the monument. Bird songs come and go
On a buffeting breeze above the slopes. A halyard
Taps and taps. Somewhere out of sight, the flag
Opens limply and folds itself again, absorbing
Thin rains that drift across the quiet hills…

'Flights nightly on the steady rising dark'

Flights nightly on the steady rising dark,
unrolling runways folding down the fields,
fields down to sea, sea into full-moon flarepath,
down all the bright to land, down all the land to night,
with its speckling path of flares and its cones of light,
we ride, and I remember the already dead,
anticipate the many still to die...
and the aircraft thunder in like Valkyries
and cut the edge of storms on the bombers' moon.

Liverpool, 1941: the stone-mason endures the blitz

My hand sandpapers on cold ribs of stone.
The pillar trembles. Eight miles to the south
in Woolton, quarrymen are sawing blocks
but here in the blitzed city, Lewis's, Church Street,
Lord Street, Salthouse, the Custom House are gone;
St Luke's, St Nick's, the Overhead, the Docks
blaze on in one huge fire beyond control.
Above me the lowering sky, appalled with smoke,
sifts charred papers in a hot, perverse snow.
Upriver, corvettes wait impatient for the oiler.
Shrapnel has scarred the south east transept wall,
splintered the shuttering, blown away the screens,
and my nails crunch across the blackened chips.
The west end's canvas sheeting flaps and cracks
in gusts of heavy air, like sails, or thunder;
the stores of dressed stone, hollowed out for shelters,
are mausoleum-cold. Dark beyond them, Hope Street's
a chaos of debris and hosepipes which my hands
long to disentangle, but I start work only
on the knots securing these tarpaulins,
hauling on clumsy sheets, my fists chapped raw
while feet skid and clatter on last night's dredge
from the nave gutters. Swollen hemps resist.
There was a dream here, thirty years the building.
The stones have fallen seven days and nights.

Akureyri

1941

The smell of chips seasons Hafnargata,
small change, while we net spring cod, and grow
accustomed to war and to our garrison, thinking
always nothing will happen. Out there
far to the north of war, Ark Royal,
they tell us, and the Hood gone down a week ago;
but the set of wind and those currents
have brought no wreckage, no reminder here;
only the half-built runway to the south
to show how things have altered
                            and the wash
where the Walrus labours off in slow pursuit
of engines now diminishing beyond the fjord
to nothing after cannon-shells and flame.
The bilges of my boat slop and spill with blood,
scaling the fish and rawly salting
our wounds. The wake unrolls to port
as we crab for home, and clouds grow north
along the valley; klipfish dry on racks;
gulls scream; while at the lieutenant's billet
in the house on the end of the spit we gather
our wounded and turn the radio on. *He'll be out of fuel
soon*, we say, telephoning farms to the east as doubt grows
into conviction: *he must be down by now*; until impossibly
too late we all hear *I have him* and a pause
before simply a *flamer* fading to dull static
then silence.

It will take us almost a week
to check his claim – until we find them both
down twenty miles away, a hundred yards apart,
wild ponies licking dope from their torn canvas.

Hjalmar Hammar

Last night, I remember after the freekirk service
so many people wishing *god nyt ar!* and shaking hands
in the luminous, drifting mist which gritted into smoke
through the rising swish and bang of New Year rockets.
how the Polar Lights bannered to shimmering green
above the blackness of the mountains to the north.

But all that fades to rumour here In this bare
and only heated room among the snows of Holandsfjordur's
January gloom. In Glomfjord, he is saying,
I have seen what we should not be able to imagine:
thirty four, he is saying, this old and gentle man,
over and over, *they shot – not just the seven workmen.*
Thirty four. Their wives. And all their children. Thirty four...
September sunlight in the slender, Arctic trees,
he is remembering, and blood. Six Germans in the squad
and then September twilight flaring phosphorescent
green before fading to pearl and this memory
above the whiteness of those mountains in the north.

Vendôme Resistance

So there was a day when they saw the troops
Scattered from seats outside the cafés
Where they had grown used to them, the uniforms
Stiffening or collapsing on drinkers
Reaching for guns among the fall of leaves,
Tables, and friends. Recounting this, one still feels blood
In the neck and ears pulsing each climax
Of fear in the square turning inside out.

Each shuttered window opens as large as the front
Of a gun. On all sides the flayed trees hide
Nothing. Six Germans are wounded, twelve dead
Even before the farmer's bicycle has stopped
Further along the gutter where he lies
Holding his face in someone else's blood:
A massacre for the Resistance to be proud of,
To make myths of. All this happens before

I am born. In fact just one man,
Armed with a rifle, got off three shots hurriedly,
Hurting no-one, not even spilling the drinks.
Sentries on every bridge sealed off the town.
By five o'clock they had him in a hotel room
With four friends. They were savagely tortured,
Then shot. Half a century later a small plaque
Asks us to think of their sacrifice.

Routed North

Blanket-clouds green down to ice-blink
in a twilight that comes to us weeping
over the top of the world. Even the sea
freezes, small floes melding into pack
as the night deepens. Where our radar says
the convoy is, we can see ghosts, ships
chalked white on the slate of the sky.
We are solid and growing, funnels rimed
where steam from the boiler condenses,
deck-housings cased by heavy seas refusing
to be water. Rails and scuppers clog with ice
when we steam-hose the gun-platforms;
davits and lifeboats transmuting to stone,
a marble frost-ship carved from arctic air.

H.M.S. Hermes   H.M.S. Sheffield

5 May 1982

Stand with me by the ski-jump, looking west.
Far out beyond our eyes' range and beyond our screen,
Something is flying in, out there where emptiness is safer;
Until, so distant that you cannot but imagine,
There blossoms one sharp, bright approaching flame. Take
    cover.
And while the thunder shakes you, you at least

Can duck. Hull down, the Sheffield burns,
Alight upon the instant, roaring beyond control;
While overhead our choppers ride assistance in the same
Clattering unsteadiness, towards the distant roll
On roll of smoke and sky and steam, below which flame
Is unimaginable now; and on our deck you'll learn

That the break in the flights of Harriers was a boy
Who will not now come home, who is not coming home
After the fatal climax of his life, after the bombing
Which took him out where he danced and died alone
And in such fire. Now turn your face to where there is
    nothing
But the cold and empty sea, dark sky, and an end of joy.

What it's been like…

airborne taxi-driver, me,
rotors mixing it hard
above a corporals' war,
Gazelle ducking and weaving
– if that doesn't sound stupid –
and last year the SAM the
bastards finally put together
screwing up out of
nowhere over bandit-country
triggered so many
on-board flaming alarms
it might have been
the Queen's fucking birthday –
but we hit the drill:
engine off, out of gear…
spin like buggery,
screaming for ground-forces
shitting theirselves laughing
at this whirlybird coming down
five hundred foot
like a spin-dried brick
– talk about wipe-out –
trim back, pitch on…
crash the sodding gears, all
the bird's inertia locking hard
into something like lift,
slowed us down, decked us out –
reaching for guns, just as the first
section hit us running: never
been so pleased to see a Rupert

three-wheel his Saracen round a corner
– just hoped the fucker
wouldn't roll it –
but now, Phil, now;
Whiterock Road
graffiti for an epitaph:
Mull of Kintyre…
Those stiffs rolling into the sea…
not clever any more.

Sergeant, A Company, First Battalion

The soldier's name has not yet been released.

When mortar shells banged closer through that night,
With you on guard and writing home to me
You managed, still, to joke about the light
You wanted out. I read that 'half-past-three'
And wondered just what time the firing ceased

In Bosnian dark. I added to my list
Of close escapes I think I know you've had:
The mine which rings your ears; the shots which missed
But rattled hard across your turret lid;

Your stumble down that cliff on mud and grease;
'The tell-tale whistle of artillery';
...a Warrior Commander badly shot...
Then silence. No news further reaches me.
I hope it's you they've wounded, hope it's not.

The soldier's name has not yet been released.

but no-one seems to be listening

Prison poems
WG 7058 HMP East York
DJH 30 YO30 6LY York

Writing together
Young Dave & Old Dave
David White & David Hughes

Young David, to his love

Today, winds tear the surface off the Ouse:
the standing-waves that slop along the bank
make foam. Above them, long, slow trains haul noise
beneath a grey, blank sky. I must not think.
Leaves fall.

And I love you.

I trace those trains in clear imaginings
to distant hills and open wilderness:
out west, at Ribblehead, where you
and I will walk, then drink and talk – and sleep –
snow drifts.

And I love you.

The Winter's setting in with cold, dark days;
and I'm closed-up in England's cul-de-sac.
In hell, we shiver, scrounging extra warmth.
Tonight where I must talk and think (and sleep)
snow lies.

And I love you.

We wait for Spring to come, to home, to York –
when trees will green along the riverbank,
and daffodils make bright the city walls;
where we will fall, and drift all day, and lie
in sunlight:

I love you.

the things I miss…

Being banged up here, of course I miss the fucking things
you all expect. Like sex: I feel so bottled up
that, in the soldier's or this prisoner's longing words,
I think, 'I must have semen coming out my ears.'
Or drink: I'd like to just get legless, now and then,
to lose myself and all the things that I've become.

Like space. I do miss distances for my bored eyes
to travel to. Or exercise: however hard
I run, it never treadmills me to somewhere else.
Like friends: a prison teaches you that no man's time
or trust can be relied upon one minute more
than satisfies his need for present company.

I don't mind noise so much: I notice only if
it stops. It never does. The prison-smell clogs in
my nose. Mass-catered food repeats its taste each week.
Here is no time to think and no time not to think,
no privacy, no room to call my own, no place
in all its crowded loneliness to be my self.

Yet this is bearable. The stuff I mostly miss
is weirder: like the smell of traffic in a queue;
those ferry-steps where fish will scarcely ever rise;
the subtle tones of someone's voice being tender; or
that touchdown hiss of settling snow on leaves, against
the screaming flanges hauling round York Station Curve.

I miss you sitting reading at our desk while I play war
games on the laptop; how the toilet door will bang
in colder, winter winds to wake us up; the way
the wardrobe quaked its way around the room and cut
across the Shipping Forecast in the early dark;
the sounds of breathing in our friendly silences.

I worry that I shall forget such things; the glow
of vodka-flambé flickering on our mince; the smoke
of candles when their flames go out; the laughter-lines
on close friends' faces at some awful joke; the way
I know you used to smell before a bath; my name
when someone speaks it to me with respect… so now…

I do not want to wait but know I must, until the day
we'll stay out walking late because we can, until
I let us in, and turn to close the loose front door;
and when you've poured the drinks we've waited for so long
you'll raise your glass and, looking at me hard, you'll find
your voice with, 'Cheers, Young David.' Then I'll know I'm
    home.

swimming in steelies

It was my self, I shakenly remember,
splashing down through night and water,
feet tight-docked in steel-toe-capped boots;
inside a numbing, fast-manacled frenzy

of thrashing legs, hands cuffed
by the heart-stopping, windpipe-cramping
shock of the freezing, too-welcoming,
river-prison, water-cell darkness

whilst ice clanged shut behind me and
the last of day blacked out; doors locked;
distant voices shouted; all the exits closed
against my dying, hopeless struggle.

* * *

It was the old man who saved me,
waiting and worried on the riverbank – alive
although his tiredness suggested otherwise –
with a fish-pole and his keep-net just in reach.

And as I hauled myself ashore, breathing hard,
snow settled cold around us like the paper
of much-read letters worn to flakes by love,
or like the fresh, white linen on the lovers' bed.

I walked home, frost-numbed by that riverside
through daylight and the un-imprisoned air,
foot-loose in trainers, home, for him to hold
to calm my fears, for him, to stop me shivering.

Cry Wolf

The darkness circles you. So often now, you've called
for help. The grown-ups think that every time they come
you let them down, and tell them lies. *The wolves are culled,*

they say. *It's safe.* And so you climb the ridge's comb
to reach your post, and cry once more that you'll be killed
by bad things lurking in the rocks. You watch a cwm

that's full of fear and night, and hide beyond the track.
You shout. Men hurry there, and do not understand
how shadows frighten you. They think it's just a trick

to get yourself attention, even though you're stunned
with dreads they can not comprehend. They turn, and trek
once more to bed. And thus, for you, the time is stained.

You're cold and tired. The light comes slow. And they're
    annoyed
so much they've said *that's it. We'll give you one more time
to tell the truth. What is it frightens you? What need?*

As if you'd know.
                    You even feel like this at home?
I ask. *I'll stay with you.*   And, though it's been denied,
yes: even there, you say. The silence of the tomb

is noise compared to this. Tonight, once more, they'll send
you out into the wilderness to guard their sheep.
You'll scream. But, knowing better, they'll ignore the sound:

he's crying wolf, like all those other times. The shape
of terror will engulf you then, as if you've sinned
so unforgivably that only Hell is sharp

enough to make you pay for all the wrong you do.
It serves him right, they'll say. *It's time he learned we won't
be running every time he yells.*   And you might die.

If only I could give you every thing that went
to heal your wounds, and made you brave. *Please: dare
to find the words you need, to tell us what you want:*

for you and I know: in the blackness there are wolves.

waiting for sentence

My life: fantasy, or reality?
I'm split between the two:
dream-scapes and harsh hell.

The rules of the jungle apply:
there's an ever-feeling of storm,
always angry and never calm.

Prison air is thick and cold.
Dreams and letters are my escape.
Without them, I don't want to wake.

Alive to everything, prepared to fight,
am I warrior or pacifist?
Do I choose to dream or to live?

Dreaming: all is surreal:
I jump from high buildings and don't die:
I am invincible.

Waking: all is surreal:
I fly on high moods and don't die:
I am invincible.

Fantasy and reality are, for me,
thoughts of being released
and living my life.

The day approaches: my time in court.
For all those here I spare no thought –
only for the dreams and lives of my closest friends

to whom I write but can rarely talk.
I watch the sun, the stars and the moon;
And pray to God for real I'll be home soon.

these things remain…

A four-inch stack of letters on our desk:
two hundred envelopes, so many words
on such strange papers, all containing kinds
of freedom written to and from my prison cell;
and looking at them now I see how much

they mattered, how I waited for your words
with so much hope, despite the fact I knew
that they would disappoint, with never quite
enough good news to rise beyond reminding me
of all that I was missing, and how much.

How did they feel to you, with their reproach
for both our faults but only me locked up;
for where you were compared with where I was?
You wrote your words from 'Home' and I from 'HMP':
two letters changed to one means very much.

My voice on tape repeating, endlessly,
defiantly, *no comment* and *no comment*, on and on,
against the interviewer's questioning
until the only comment I have made's the knife itself
in both our memories and in the Ouse.

And all the other letters: those you sent
To anyone you thought or hoped could help.
You said, *I'm kicking doors and banging desks.*

Although I'm lost for words I'm shouting too,
but even now I fear there's no-one listening…

It's time for you to be my Simon Yates

I know what rope means to you:
        assurance, security, anchor,
                guide, handline, safeguard.

You have roped many people,
        leading them to good places,
                keeping safe in the dangerous ones.

You used a rope of sorts to haul me out of trouble
        more than once – a rope of words.
                We've shared a rope of hemp now and then.

But, at last, it has come to this:
        for as long as you tie me in to these coils
            you strangle me.

Your rope holds me back
        on routes I must climb on my own.
                It pulls me off-line in dangerous places.
                    It will make me fall.

And if we are tied together like this, we will fall
        together like this, probably die together
            like this. Do not forget.
                It will be the end of us.

I know that you have done this thing before.
        You know that I know:
                Long afterwards, I toasted his memory.

I do understand.
        I know what it might cost.
                Do it again. For me. Now.
                        Cut the fucking rope.

If I climb, I'll be great.
        If I fall, I'll be okay.
                If I'm not, it won't be your fault.

Remember:
        You set me free.
                Let yourself go as well.

If this succeeds
        we'll be together, though unroped
                everywhere, free, together.

an *Airwalk* bag on a wheelchair back

1.

Once I had seen the bag itself, and the logo,
and heard him say *I wish that I could walk*
I can't remember what I noticed next: but still…
The quantities of longings and of lunch that bag contained.

His carer stooped over him to tell him *so do I*, in the sun
   and the rain
and signals changed ahead of us, unblocking the pavement
in Museum Street where two vehicles halted at a red light
and stopped me too: the first, a transfer-ambulance

of handicapped young people, recognising me, waving:
and then a prison van, black window squares behind which
   too
there were people, surely, waving in the sun and at the rain.
I hear them saying *I wish that I could walk*. I want to tell
   them also *so do I*.

II.

We did see each other – though not nearly often enough –
and all of our visits ended the same way, with each of us
walking to places the other one could not imagine
although we did try every time; and then there were times
when we both of us found us in tears that we knew we'd not
   share
until our next swapping of letters, or not even then.

The road seemed so cold when I left you to go into sun set;
And I did not dare to look back to the pillars of salt, or to
   think of you
all of the time I was wishing your freedom, and thinking
about you and how you must feel I betrayed you by leaving;
and thought of you thinking of me going further away then,
even from meetings we both knew were bringing us close.

Your Wing was much louder, as I used to think, so much
   colder
and darker, whatever the lights they put up all the time,
while you might be thinking of bang-up and dinner, or sleep;
but with nowhere else you could go to or wander about;
and never to think you could walk away free by yourself
out to places you thought of as home, or wherever you
   wanted.

* * *

Then slowly the distance between us began not to matter
as we came to think, as we thought all the more of each other;
and who was the more or less captive in those times and places
we do not believe we are sure or can know, even now.

And the wheelchair back? and the Airwalk *bag? Well, think*
    about them:
like poetry, really: the things a word means in its place.

Matthew Hatton, RIP

from Young David

It is not because I knew you, but I know the ones who did:
I understand the vacancy you leave in many lives.
But, we know you told your sisters not to sadden. What you
    said
is, you loved what you were doing. And this is what
    survives,

the first family photograph:
a boy outside York Minster: marching in a Scout's uniform,
St George's Day Parade,
flags in the background;

the Silence of the Desert:
explosions screaming amongst the rocks;
army boots running, stones crunching;
soldiers eating, drinking and weeping;
the Last Post sounding;
every noise mournful:
every one calling for you…

the Silence of the City:
owls *who-whoo?*-ing among the trees;
a siren keening over Lendal;
the Ouse splashing by towpaths and reeds;
Great Peter tolling;
every noise mournful:
every one calling for you…

the second family photograph:
a man outside York Minster: carried in a Soldier's coffin,
your Funeral Parade,
flags in the foreground.

If you are looking down at this, you must think that you are
    dreaming.
My friends would tell you: normally, I am not a man who
    cries,
but today below York Minster steps I find my tears are
    streaming.
There must be grits of sand, blown in from Helmand, in my
    eyes.

Autumn

Last year, whilst you kicked your heels in Hull, I kicked
     autumn into heaps
which were golden in sunlight. I wanted to send you
     reminders of our riverbank,
in the sound of those colours, the fragile textures of vein
     and leaf,

damp scents of their decay as they slopped into mulch after
     rain.
I could not do it. Prison screws at best would have thought
     them unclean;
at worst they would surely be looked on as something
     narcotic to smoke.

I closed a few in laminate, trying to fix them in time for
     you, for later.
This year, together, we watch sycamore seeds helicoptering
     off, down
towards winter, biding their own time, finding their places,
     waiting to become.

The Two Corbies

Just there beyond the old full dyke
I know there lies a new-slain knight;
And nobody knows that he lies there
But his hawk, his hound, and lady fair.

Oh yes, the ballad makes me think of hooded crows,
or 'hoodies' in the *Lallans*. Awkwardly, yours comes to mind,
or mine as it was, the grey fleece which I lent you that first time
they came to arrest you, for some ridiculous bomb hoax.

You'll sit on his white neck bone,
And I'll pick out his bonny blue eyes;
And with a lock of his golden hair
We'll thicken our nest when it grows bare.

No scuffer thought to take the draw-string from its neck
although you might have hanged yourself in their cell,
where you would have found an anchor had you chose,
my young unslain, fair-haired knight of the blue eyes.

Many a one for him makes moan,
But none shall know where he is gone;
Over his white bones, when they we bare,
The wind shall blow for evermore.

I see an air-raid hoodie, no bones. Boy, you were twelve
in Hiroshima that fine August morning, no hoax. Yours too
has a neck-tie. Its close-weave silk seems utterly undamaged.
Nobody knows now under which hot wind or ditch you lay.

I hear two 'hoodies' making moan;
The one unto the other say
'Where shall we go and dine today?'
As I am walking all alone.

Tornado

I bet against old Dave: I wrote, *when I get out,*
I'll do this too. Till then, show me how good you are:
draw me Tornado *in the roundhouse – in her paint –*
or on the track. Dave took the bait. A cross-hatched sketch
came folded back, her shining tender apple-green
behind the pencil, as my tutor rightly said. And I,
inside my cell, imagined steam, and loudly heard
the screeling sound of flanges from the wheels which would
one day be taking both of us to somewhere else.

Dave met me and we took a train from HMP to Leeds.
Well, that was strange enough. Dave knew he'd leave me
　　there
with both of us not knowing when we'd meet again –
but, stranger still, next day I did meet Dave in town
and after that, he walked me to the station where
I'd catch another train to meet my family.

There's something not enough with this word *meet:*
it won't discriminate between the times we all intend
and those we find by accident – but then, it makes
you wonder if it's *meant.* While crossing Scarborough Bridge
we scent the steam, and hear the hiss of cylinders:
Tornado's here, drawn up along a crowded Platform Ten –
and this is *her* first trip with paying passengers,
and here I am with Dave, high on York Station Bridge.

At noon, with perfect timing, north *Tornado* goes
– *chuff* – *chuff* – I wish I could *express* it so – with sun
-light on her boiler, on her steam.　　And I am free.

top of the flood

I know I have backed-off from this all day
by looking somewhere else, at water, geese,
or sodden river debris settling on the line
where thoughts don't want to stray: to not
be thinking how the knife-scar chills my throat;
yet, in today's cold wind, the cut they closed
and tabbed with steri-strips, recalls for me…

but *no*: that's *not* exactly what they said.
I'll spell it out: *sterr ee oh strips*, as if
to make it feel more three dimensional…
and read what young Dave wrote: 'I chose the knife:
I knew how blunt it was: I didn't mean
to cut his throat, just frighten him.' Well, that's
why I insist that they were steri-strips, for Dave,

to show how clean it was. I've cut myself
much worse just shaving – if you can believe
old memories – but that's not every thing:
I speak to David in the kitchen or his chair
and silence answers me with all those words
we never used to say but wanted to.
I buy the kinds of food I think he would,

and spice it up, and cook as if for him.
We write our letters, which expand the notes
we used to leave each other unexplained.
I read the books and poems which we know
and share and both enjoy: so Edward Thomas's
The Gallows speaks to us, as does my own,
the first for us: *winds tear the surface off the Ouse…*

upon which he will swim, and I find calm:
these covenants which tell me all will pass:
and no more violence disturb our flesh…
it's strange: it's not his absence shaking me
but that he's waiting here with me thus patiently
to spend our nights and all our days to come; and so
I know how much it's all alright between us now.

Low Expectations

Indeed, it was Dickensian, although the stories got us all-
    mixed-up;
so the only place to sleep was the prison-hangman's burial-
    ground,
wet, dank, and gloomy in a freezing, river-long, pre-
    Christmas fog.
Safe enough though: it's not the kind of place that any one'd
    ever choose
to wander into in the dark, however drunk they were; an'
    far too cold
for even lookin' out for casual sex at the end of a night on
    the lash.

Yet there I was, sleeping-bagged, warm in the under-
    shadow of arc-lights,
sheltered by headstones. Come dawn, I loomed from the
    mist like Magwitch.
And sure, I would have put a healthy fear of God up any
    Sunday passers-by,
hauling myself out, grey and stiff, from tree-roots and the
    tumbling monuments.
But you, my Pip, you were a convict still, an' banged-up on
    the wronger side
of yon' high prison wall. There were no chance-meetings for
    us. Not like last night

when I were mugged. 'You, what 'r' you doin' out 'ere, this
    hour i' the mornin'?'
I felt like my teenaged-self, with all that I could not explain;
    and I was so much
afraid of losing my phone and the cash and my wallet,
    although the 'return'

I had hid in the sole of my shoe should at least get me
    home. Of course, I tried:
'eddin' for 'eddon Road, dahn the prison. I'm goan' out there
    to see me mate.'
'At effin' two o'clock in the effin' mornin', he sezz, 'what *are*
    you effin' on about?'

'Christmas,' I say. 'I've got to see mi mate inside: I can't not
    go to him, not now;
an' tomorrow mornin' is the only visit-slot that they got left.
    So here I am. Walkin'.'
'Well, bugger me,' he says, wiv me still full of fright, an' 'im
    reachin' out to grab me,
twistin' me round so I looks at him, holdin' me hard, an'
    starin' me into mi eyes –
the while I'm thinkin', 'Here it comes.' And I wonder,
    'when'll they find me? Where?'
'Tekk this,' he says, and he thrusts me forty quid. 'Mekk sure
    you pass it on.'

That lad became Tolkein-ian, our Striding Ghost of
    Christmas Present. Who he was
or what he meant by that, no need for us to want to know. I
    almost doubt if, drunken,
he remembers us, Pip. But you and me and the visiting
    room, we were transformed.

And me? well, if I'd only not tripped-up on a tree-root after,
    fetchin' mi bag, an' splittin'
me head on a tombstone, getting' the bloodiest wound of
    the whole bloody saga.
But still, it's true: I am looking forward to sharing wi' you a
    Blacksmith's pie an' pint.

Matthew 25: The sheep tells it as he sees it

So, You, the Son of Man, is this my proper seat or not? – on
    your right hand?
You're sure it's not a trick? You really caught me by surprise
    just now,
by quoting Matthew on St Martin's Day, and listing all the
    good I've done.

Aye, David was an hungred, so I gave him meat; but
    nothing fancy, not a lot;
leftovers really, or would have been. As for the drink, I'd
    rather share a pint
than sup alone with just a book. I liked his company, bright
    lad, good talker;

which meant that when I took him in he wasn't quite a
    stranger, more a friend.
And, yes, I gave him clothes: it was midwinter, after all, and
    he'd been on the streets.
Cast-offs they were, not much to me, foul-weather stuff I'd
    never wear again.

Of course I went to visit him in gaol. What else? You know
    he'd no-one else.
Perhaps, though, that was where I failed. I couldn't set him
    free, the way I fed
and watered, housed and clothed him. All in all, it still don't
    seem like much.

But if You say so, I suppose it's true: turns out I'm not a
    goat: I haven't failed

to help your 'least of these'. I didn't not-do things I should
   have done.
                  Hold on!
You've got me where you want me now: the sin of Pride. I'll
   sit the other side.

Matthew 25: and the goat responds

What's this about then, Christ? – you calling me *one of the*
     least of these. Why?
Last thing I thought you said, *we are all equal in the sight of*
     God. What changed?
If you'd said *in the sight of Man* I would know what you
     meant – those sheep
who look across at us if we're here to prove that they're the
     best, to take their charity.

Well, yes, I did feel gratitude; though the more I think about
     it now, the more I'm sure
that *getting* matters just as much as *giving.* I think about the
     food he gave me first:
leftovers, cold: he never thought to ask if I'd got likes or
     dislikes, stuff like that.
The pints were fair enough, although it still seems right that
     what I drank was bitter.

Leftover clothes, him clearing shelves to make himself feel
     good, nothing matching,
no sense of fitting *me* so much as they no longer fitted him.
     Ungracious of me
to refuse them, though. And winter, so I had no real choice
     – like, when he said
he'd take me in, my *please* and *thank you* kept me off the
     freezing streets,

and kept his conscience clear. Mind you, he was good
     hearted too, he really was,
thinking of me even when the lad whom he imagined
     wasn't me, not exactly 'me'.

It's just the prison stretch annoys me now. Of course he
    came to see me there,
kindly enough, but then we both knew he'd provoked me till
    he put me there.

So think on this: could he have given stuff without someone
    to take it from him?
– to be grateful for it, even when it didn't suit or fit, to take
    it when my instinct said

Stuff this?

No, I don't want no credit from you, Christ. I shouldn't have
    complained.
Perhaps You got it right: I feel that I belong among the least
    of these. I wish…

'Late this evening in a war'

Late this evening in a war
That has lasted thirty years,
Amusing myself by rewatching
Old news, I am surprised
By the shock of my young face filmed
Above the wick of a petrol bomb
Starting to catch and flare and light me
Like a scare-game played with torches.
Making childish monsters in the dark I
Frighten myself. How well this picture
Fixes me then for thirty years for ever.

'My life has been'

My life has been
cold mountain.

The paths of my going
and of my coming
are loose on the clatter
of scree still
finding its angle.

I drink water
cooled by melt
or poured steadily
from clouds that weep
the grey sorrow
of their clinging

stained with rock
and stone ground small
by the slow anger
of fallen snow.

My food tastes
of coarse grass
nibbled by sheep.
I breathe thin air.

Barn Owl

I saw you tonight,
passing like a ghost on the dark hill,
in dusk hovering and into dark pouncing
to a noise beyond the wall on the far moor
that some would say the cat from this farm, or
the farm on the next hill, made.

I thought it was you.
And from the night other noises:
the squeal and white flash of the startled plover
on the field before me,
and the curlew's bubble in the night sky.
In torchlight I checked you in the book:
and 'it must be you', I thought, 'no cat
ever shrieked or hissed like that,
on the farm or on the hill
or in the town in my hearing
– except the one I see now on the wall
behind bright eyes and torchlight
and the same shrieking and hissing and all that.'

The noise was not you;
but at least I can say,
At least I saw you today.

Owl

for Justin Clark

I drank with you, and walked for miles, talking
of nothing or of anything; of birds:
those rooks along the crop-line; skylark song;

that kestrel close above the lane ahead,
stooping on unseen rodents; chaffinches.
Not long before I left, you said, 'Last night

I thought of owls. I'm not sure why: perhaps
the dusk, or the full moon. *Exactly then
one came across the hedge – as if it knew.*'

* * *

Your owl's much more than 'bird of wisdom' now:
it calls along my days like memory,
or smoke which re-assembles its solidity,

or flame that shrinks to kindling, branches, logs.
It roosts in trees whose foliage strips down
to drift and leaf-mould, humus for the spring.

It haunts those barns which crumble from neglect
back into earth, where spores spin up through beams
of light, or timber, ready to begin.

'Prepared early'

Prepared early,
got together food and other sustenance
– warm clothing, shelter –
and planned my expeditions well.

Went alone at first:
spent many days exploring
moorland, bleak and featureless;
here and there finding small brilliance
– the bright, carnivorous sundew
surprisingly at the pathside,
trodden beneath all eyes,
unnoticed, fine, worth watching;
or on the grey line of the horizon,
small wayguides, ancient landmarks,
eye-catching, re-assuring, strongholds of memory –

Then graduated to the higher lands,
saw the sun rise above flooding clouds,
slept close beneath the stars;
held my balance on sharp, spectacular uplands;
my own life
at the cwm's rim
or on the steep
escarpment's sudden edge.

Becoming competent, having the scenery mapped,
began to guide others.

I'd like to take you with me all the way.

Scarborough – Whitby

June 1990

It seemed enough: to walk for hours along the coast
A week before the shortest night, beneath a sky
Which darkened in the offshore wind by chill degrees –
Until, at dawn, we felt a huge, transcendent sense:
How all of earth's and ocean's edges might roll down,
When all the brilliant eastern water scooped up light
From that small, trembling, cloud-occluded disc
And flooded it at us, and lit the land behind.

Y.R.C. Lowstern

1 Jan 1994

I had remembered sound and silence this New Year:
Their laughter growing with a board game's each success;
The stillness into which a blackbird's chinking call
Fell, through last year's last dusk; the generator's beat
Which followed us up Ingleborough's flank; the wind
Whose crystals sibilantly brushed my chilling face;
The distant diesel of those trains which pull their slow
Selves east and west along the dale; the broadcast bells
At midnight, chiming through our champagne's fizz and
    splash;

Until the year's first sun goes down in front of me,
And I perceive across the sky's grey, laden height
How light has poured its self into these hills, these days,
Its clarity, its own simplicity fine drawn
In dashes of snow's purity: its promises.

Bearing Gifts

I am driving west for Christmas,
towards the M40, Oxford ahead of me.
In my mirror a full moon hangs
low over London, and the radio
murmurs on without distraction

except for the News. Poland
has Military Rulers, and Christmas,
foodless under steady snow,
is in doubt. There is rioting
in Gdansk, and in Katowice small groups

resist the Militia hopelessly;
but I am untouched until at Uxbridge
I pass the eagled column, for Polish airmen
forty years ago defending us. Overhead
white contrails drift in blue September skies

while I think eastwards where others alone
or in convoy travel bearing gifts.
The sun clouds, then sets; and my headlamps
light on flakes suddenly rising in the arc
of wipers. I queue at every junction.